Contemporary Musicians
AND THEIR MUSIC™

My Chemical Romance

Laura La Bella

ROSEN
PUBLISHING
New York

Published in 2009 by The Rosen Publishing Group, Inc.
29 East 21st Street, New York, NY 10010

Library of Congress Cataloging-in-Publication Data

La Bella, Laura.
My Chemical Romance / Laura La Bella.—1st ed.
    p. cm.—(Contemporary musicians and their music)
Includes bibliographical references and index.
ISBN-13: 978-1-4042-1818-5 (library binding)
ISBN-13: 978-1-4358-5126-9 (pbk)
ISBN-13: 978-1-4042-7871-4 (6 pack)
1. My Chemical Romance (Musical group)—Juvenile literature. 2. Rock musicians—United States—Biography—Juvenile literature. I. Title.
ML3930.M97L3 2008
782.42166092'2—dc22
[B]

                                                        2008007130

Manufactured in Malaysia

On the cover: Pictured here are the band members of My Chemical Romance.

Contents

Introduction

Gerard Way, the lead singer of the indie rock/punk band My Chemical Romance, was working as a graphic designer at the Cartoon Network in New York City in the fall of 2001. When he arrived at work on September 11, Way had no idea that, by the day's end, the world would change and he would make a life-changing decision.

That fall day in New York is forever linked in Americans' minds as a day the country endured a paralyzing terrorist attack. But for Way, the day marked a beginning. It was the day he decided he

The members of My Chemical Romance pose for a photo session in Germany to promote their tour. The band's members are *(left to right)* Frank Iero, Ray Toro, Gerard Way, Bob Bryar, and Mike Way.

would start a band. Witnessing the planes crash into the World Trade Center, he felt an overwhelming urge to do something meaningful with his life. Within days, he quit his job and wrote his first song, "Skylines and Turnstiles," which expressed his feelings about September 11.

The drive to make a difference fueled Way to bring together a group of childhood friends to form My Chemical Romance. The band—Gerard and Michael Way, Matt Pelissier, Ray Toro, and Frank Iero—were all natives of New Jersey. They set out to record their debut album, *I Brought You My Bullets, You Brought Me Your Love*, for Eyeball Records, a small but influential independent record company. The album drew the attention of Reprise Records, which signed the band to its first major record deal. Multiple tours and albums followed as the band developed a legion of fans, both in the United States and around the world.

As five guys from the "wrong" side of Jersey, they found success playing to crowds of young kids looking to relate to a version of themselves. The band found a loyal following in other lost souls who appreciated their scary, sad, emotionally charged version of punk rock. Gerard Way described to *Rolling Stone* magazine how he'd always viewed My Chemical Romance: "As the band that would have represented who me and my friends were in high school, and the band that we didn't have to represent us—the kids that wore black—back then."

Influenced by legendary bands like Queen and Iron Maiden, My Chemical Romance produced theatrical albums that captured the drama of life. And their live shows were no different. On stage, My Chemical Romance played concerts around the world, and they loved playing for their fans. Their shows were theatrical, enthusiastic, and rich with passion and energy. The shows were the very embodiment of the band itself. Way would have it no other way.

Chapter One

Jersey Boys

Belleville is a small, working-class township in Essex County, New Jersey. Located on the Passaic River, not far from New York City, the town has produced some legendary performers over the years and has received some unusual popularity, thanks to the television show *The Sopranos* and the Tony Award–winning Broadway musical *Jersey Boys*.

HBO's mob drama *The Sopranos* used a number of Belleville locations to film scenes during the show's ten-season run. Several notable locations, including the Rail Road Bridge, have been featured in the show's opening credits. Most recently, Belleville was featured in *Jersey Boys*, the Broadway musical that follows the rise and fall of Frankie Valli and the Four Seasons, a famous American pop group from the mid-1960s. The group's members,

Valli, Bob Gaudio, Nick Massi, and Tommy DeVito, all grew up in Belleville. The town was also a location for the 2001 Oscar-winning film *A Beautiful Mind.*

For Gerard and Michael "Mikey" Way, Belleville was the beginning of a journey that would take these two brothers—and their friends from the neighborhood—around the world.

Gerard Way was born on April 9, 1977. His brother, Mikey, joined the family three years later, on September 10, 1980. The brothers grew up in one of Belleville's roughest neighborhoods and were forced to stay indoors as much as possible to avoid the crime in the neighborhood. "Me and Mikey couldn't really play where we grew up, which was pretty much the same story as everybody, because it was so . . . dangerous," Gerard Way told *Alternative Press* in an interview.

Gerard Way *(right)*, lead singer of My Chemical Romance, is photographed hanging out in the outdoor backstage area while on the 2005 Vans Warped Tour.

"We had to construct our own world we lived in constantly." As a result, the brothers amused themselves by reading comic books, watching cartoons, and playing board and role-playing games like Dungeons and Dragons.

Working hard to provide for them, their father, Donald, was a service manager at a car dealership, and their mother, Donna, was a hairdresser. Because the Ways were too scared to let their children play outside, the brothers developed a deep bond early. "We didn't have anyone else to hang out with," Mikey Way explained to *Alternative Press*. "We had friends from the neighborhood, but it was mostly me and Gerard."

Surviving School

Their parents didn't have records or a radio, and they didn't listen to music. In fact, there was no music at all in the Way home. But thanks to the influence of their grandmother, Elena "Helena" Lee Rush, both boys developed an interest in music. Rush even encouraged Gerard Way to audition for the lead role in his school's fourth-grade production of *Peter Pan*.

"My grandmother was my main connection to art and music," he told *Rolling Stone* magazine in an interview. "She could play piano very well, and she had perfect pitch. She's the one who pushed me to try out for *Peter Pan*, and I ended up getting the part. When I tried out, I realized I could sing, which was pretty interesting."

Gerard Way worked as a bagger in a grocery store and as a clerk in a comic book store while he was in high school. After he graduated, he attended college at the School of Visual Arts in New York City, where he majored in cartooning/illustration and developed his interest in the arts. After graduation, he took his portfolio around and searched for a job as a cartoon animator. But his interest in music was also strong. He was influenced by the rock, alternative, hardcore, and heavy metal bands of the 1980s and 1990s, like the Misfits, Black Flag, Descendants, Pantera, At the Gates, the Cure, and the Smiths. Two bands in particular had expressive frontmen who intrigued him: Iron Maiden's Bruce Dickinson and Thursday's Geoff Rickly.

"[Dickinson] really inspired me 'cause he's a great frontman, a great singer, and I've always been influenced by the way he sang," Way said in an interview with MetalUnderground.com. "Also, Geoff from Thursday inspired me as a person to just get up and do that. I've been a fan of music and I've always wanted to be in a band. I just never had the urge to be a frontman until I saw him do it. It just seems like he's actually making a

An early influence on My Chemical Romance is Bruce Dickinson, the lead singer of the heavy metal band Iron Maiden. Gerard Way called Dickinson "a great frontman" and counted him among the best singers in heavy metal music.

difference and he was doing something."

Meanwhile, Mikey Way, who shared his brother's interest in music, finished high school and was going to college part-time while working at Barnes & Noble Booksellers. While he loved music, he had no clear career direction. He did, however, intern at Eyeball Records, a move that would be very important for the brothers down the road.

A Nation Is Changed, a Band Is Born

Gerard Way's life was at a standstill, and he was slipping into a deep depression in the late summer and early fall of 2001. Then, on September 11, he was jolted out of his rut. As the nation watched footage of two planes crashing into the World Trade

The 9/11 terrorist attacks on the World Trade Center changed Gerard Way's life. From that moment on, he felt compelled to make a difference in the world and find a connection to others. Within weeks, he established his band, My Chemical Romance.

Center, Way witnessed the events unfold through the windows of the Cartoon Network's offices in downtown New York City.

"Something just clicked in my head that morning," he told *Spin* magazine. "I literally said to myself, 'I've gotta get out of the basement. I've gotta see the world. I've gotta make a difference.'"

Within days, he wrote a song, "Skylines and Turnstiles," inspired by September 11. That week, he placed a call to his friend, Matt Pelissier, a drummer he knew from high school. He and Pelissier met up at a local club, the Loop Lounge.

"I ran into Matt at a bar and said, 'You know what? I've been writing songs. You're not doing anything, I'm not doing anything, so let's get together and give it a shot,'" Way told *Alternative Press* magazine.

At the 2005 MTV Video Music Awards, Matt Pelissier of My Chemical Romance arrives at the American Airlines Arena in Miami, Florida.

Pelissier added some drum tracks to Way's rough first version of "Skylines and Turnstiles." The two became the first official members of the band. A few days later, Way called Ray Toro, a film student from their neighborhood in Belleville, and asked him to join the band as its lead guitarist. At the time, Way couldn't sing and play the guitar at the same time.

The band made its first recordings in Pelissier's attic. "I had a really cheap 16-track board and we had a bunch of [lousy] mics," Pelissier told *Alternative Press*. "I basically had the drums and guitars playing upstairs and ran mics down the stairs and had Gerard sing in the bathroom." Those rough music sessions led to the band's first three songs: "Skylines and Turnstiles," "Our Lady of Sorrows" (formerly called "Bring More Knives"), and "Cubicles."

"You could hear it was something really new, and it was kind of a weird idea, but for some reason, as poorly as it was coming together, it really worked," Way told *Alternative Press*, describing the band's first experience recording. While rough around the edges, the demo brought the band some early attention. Everyone who heard the songs loved them, including Mikey. When Gerard's younger brother heard the demo, he promptly dropped out of college, took up the bass guitar—an instrument he had never played before—and joined the band.

As the four band members continued to write songs and rehearse together, bonding over their difficult childhoods on the rough streets of urban New Jersey, they refined their sound. The band paired uphappy lyrics with upbeat music, creating an outlet for their anger and angst. They now had a way to scream about the world, while also saying something intelligent and expressing their feelings. For Gerard Way, it was a much-needed release.

The band, however, still needed a name. Inspired by the book *Ecstasy: Three Tales of Chemical Romance* by author Irvine Welsh, Mikey Way came up with the name My Chemical Romance. He would later tell *Spin* magazine, "[The band] always had a vision, but we weren't sure if it would translate or just come off as pretentious."

Chapter Two

My Chemical Romance Courts Its Audience

As they wrote more songs and became comfortable playing together, My Chemical Romance started to perform in and around New Jersey, often playing at parties held in friends' basements. Their sound—a mix of pop rock infused with heavy metal and featuring moving, often tumultuous lyrics—appealed to fans. The band quickly built an impressive fan base. It didn't take long before they met the right people and had a record deal in place.

Playing Dates Around Jersey

My Chemical Romance played anyplace they could. At the time, a lot of bands played house parties and in basements. Geoff Rickly, lead singer of the band Thursday, threw a number of basement parties and often invited My Chemical Romance to play. Those early parties were a way to keep the focus on the music and bring it to a mass of young kids eager to hear the next big thing.

Another person interested in hearing the newest music was Alex Saavedra, a fixture on the New Jersey music scene. Saavedra was the founder and owner of Eyeball Records. He—along with the heads of other independent New Jersey record labels, like Chuck Kinahan and Derek Meier of On the Rise Records and Jason Small of XOXO Records—played a pivotal role in helping New Jersey become a hotbed for underground, independent label (indie) music. As important as Seattle was to the grunge movement in rock, which produced such notable bands as Nirvana and Pearl Jam, New Jersey was the breeding ground for bands in the so-called punk revival movement. New Jersey was producing some amazing punk rock bands, like Thursday and Pencey Prep—both signed to Saavedra's label.

Mikey Way happened to be interning for Eyeball Records, where he carried equipment, posted fliers for bands, and did whatever needed to be done for the label. His internship gave the band the perfect opportunity to hang out with Saavedra.

Saavedra was known to throw house parties almost every weekend, inviting bands to play and often signing the ones he liked to Eyeball Records. One night, Mikey gave Saavedra a copy

To promote its album, My Chemical Romance joined the 2007 Projekt Revolution Tour. Here, guitarist Frank Iero plays during a sold-out concert stop in California.

of the demo tape My Chemical Romance had recorded in Pelissier's attic. After hearing the band's demo tape, Saavedra signed the band immediately.

It was at Eyeball Records, in one of their recording studios, that My Chemical Romance was introduced to the fifth member of their band. Frank Iero was the onetime lead vocalist and guitarist for Pencey Prep, an indie rock band. Pencey Prep was breaking up, and Iero was looking for a new band to play with. My Chemical Romance signed him on as a guitarist just days before the band recorded its debut album. It proved to be an important move for the band.

A student at Rutgers University, Iero had played not only for Pencey Prep but also for Hybrid, Sector 12, I Am a Graveyard, and Give Up the Ghost. He had experience playing live, which was something the rest of the band lacked. Iero's concert knowledge would become invaluable when the band eventually booked live shows other than basement parties.

A Debut Album

In early 2002, My Chemical Romance, Saavedra, and Rickly drove up to Nada Studios in North Windsor, New York, and began recording *I Brought You My Bullets, You Brought Me Your Love.*

Currently, Nada Studios is a major recording venue, but back then, John Naclerio, Nada's owner, was still working out of his mother's basement.

"As soon as it came time for Gerard to do vocals for 'Vampires Will Never Hurt You,' this insane storm hit," Saavedra recalled in an interview with *Alternative Press*. "Gerard was getting very frustrated because it was his first time recording, decently, in an

My Chemical Romance is voted Favorite Band by fans in Who's Next?, an online showcase where users select their favorite band. The contest was sponsored by LAUNCH, the music destination on Yahoo!, and by Saturn.

actual studio. He was overwhelmed and he was over-thinking it."
So, Saavedra did something unusual: he punched Gerard Way.

"I remember thinking it hurt a lot, and going, 'All right, I hope
I can do this,'" Way told *Alternative Press*. "I remember singing,
and something clicked. I remember Alex's face was just amazed
that the song was finally coming together. I think it was the
second take that we ended up using."

Just three months after forming, My Chemical Romance had
finished its debut album. The group was often compared to the
band Thursday due to the many similarities between the two
groups. Both hailed from New Jersey, both recorded for Eyeball
Records, and both combined pop's upbeat propulsion with
introspective, confessional lyrics. And, of course, Thursday's
lead vocalist was Geoff Rickly, who produced the *Bullets* album.

Bullets was released on July 23, 2002, to favorable reviews.
Alex Henderson, of All Music Guide, described the album as
emotionally charged. "*I Brought You My Bullets, You Brought Me
Your Love* is a generally decent effort—one that deals with a lot
of negative emotions and does so in a very candid way. Some
will find the lyrics depressing, but then, rock music isn't obliged
to press the smile button 24 hours a day . . . It's a noteworthy,
generally respectable debut for a New Jersey combo."

MAKING TRACKS

I Brought You My Bullets, You Brought Me Your Love is My Chemical Romance's debut album. Released on July 23, 2002, the album was produced by Thursday's lead singer, Geoff Rickly, and includes the following tracks:

- "Romance"
- "Honey, This Mirror Isn't Big Enough for the Two of Us"
- "Vampires Will Never Hurt You"
- "Drowning Lessons"
- "Our Lady of Sorrows"
- "Headfirst for Halos"
- "Skylines and Turnstiles"
- "Early Sunsets Over Monroeville"
- "This Is the Best Day Ever"
- "Cubicles"
- "Demolition Lovers"

The album features Gerard Way's September 11–inspired song, "Skylines and Turnstiles." And many of the album's other song titles deal with similarly poignant topics, such as "Vampires Will Never Hurt You." Henderson noted in his All Music Guide review: "Like so many angst-ridden alternative pop/rock and punk-pop artists who have emerged in the early 2000s, My Chemical Romance knows how to be exuberant and introspective at the same time—musically, they tend to be aggressive and hard rocking, but lyrically, they're all about introspection."

Chapter Three

A Major-Label Deal

To promote *I Brought You My Bullets, You Brought Me Your Love*, My Chemical Romance began playing bars and clubs around New Jersey, which led to its first big break. Brian Schechter, a tour manager, caught the band's performance one night and immediately thought the band would be perfect to open for the Used. My Chemical Romance signed with Schechter, who eventually became the band's manager.

Bullets eventually grabbed the attention of Reprise Records, a major label connected with Warner Bros. Records, which signed My Chemical Romance in 2003. Soon, the band members began work on their second album, *Three Cheers for Sweet Revenge*.

Mainstream Success

Released in 2004, *Three Cheers for Sweet Revenge* went platinum, selling a million copies, within a year. The band released three singles from the album: "I'm Not Okay (I Promise)," "Helena," and "The Ghost of You." It was produced by Howard Benson, who had gained a solid reputation for his work with such groups as Papa Roach, P.O.D., Hoobastank, and the All-American Rejects.

Describing its sound, Gerard Way says the band finds inspiration and influence from an earlier era of rock. "A big inspiration for us goes back to the glam era, where there was an element of theater involved in rock and roll," he told *Rolling Stone*. "We love bands like Queen, where it's huge and majestic, but also bands like Black Flag and the Misfits, who would go absolutely crazy."

Three Cheers for Sweet Revenge was semi-autobiographical. In an interview with the *New York Times*, Way explained the album's theme. "*Three Cheers* is a concept album about a man who comes back from the dead to [haunt] people who shut him out for not fitting in during his lifetime. The band lent itself to that sort of thing. All of us grew up as geeks, getting picked on and being told we weren't good enough."

The album also represented the band's loyal fans, many of whom felt like outcasts themselves. In an interview with *Rolling Stone*, Way described the band's fans as extremely creative, intelligent, expressive, and very individual. "They come from all over the place, and in their hometown they're probably the only kid who looks like that, but when they get to our show they're all the same. One of the best compliments I can get from one of them is, 'I met my best friend at one of your shows,' or, 'I met my best friend networking on the Internet, trying to get to your show.' That's cool, because I didn't have that," he said.

A reviewer for *Rolling Stone* gave the album three stars, writing, "My Chemical Romance embrace the goth-punk revival in style. Thanks to frontman Gerard Way's endearing warble, standout tracks such as 'Helena' and 'I'm Not Okay (I Promise)' come off as more emotion-driven than shock rock. In any case, *Revenge* is a [heck] of a good time."

Many critics agreed. Garnering a spate of positive reviews, *Three Cheers for Sweet Revenge* created a stir upon its release. The album landed in the number 1 position on Billboard's Heatseeker chart, at number 28 on the Billboard 200 album chart, and at number 103 on the Top Internet Album chart. The

Touring the world to support their album *Three Cheers for Sweet Revenge*, My Chemical Romance's lead singer Gerard Way *(left)* and guitarist Ray Toro perform at the San Jose State Event Center in San Jose, California.

album's first single, "I'm Not Okay (I Promise)," peaked at number 4 on Billboard's Modern Rock Tracks, number 64 on the Pop 100, and number 86 on the Hot 100 chart.

The album's second single, "Helena," was a tribute to Gerard and Mickey's grandmother, who passed away in 2003, while the brothers were on tour. The song's lyrics describe Gerard Way's feelings for his late grandmother. The song peaked at number 13 on Billboard's Hot Digital Songs chart, number 11 on the

Modern Rock Tracks chart, number 31 on the Pop 100 chart, and number 33 on the Hot 100 chart. The song was also used to close the band's shows each night when they were on tour.

The album's third single, "The Ghost of You," peaked at number 38 on Billboard's Mainstream Rock Tracks chart, number 9 on the Modern Rock Tracks chart, number 78 on the Pop 100 chart, and number 84 on the Hot 100 chart.

The band embarked on the Vans Warped Tour '04, a two-month, fifty-city tour featuring more than thirty bands. Playing around the country, My Chemical Romance gained fans everywhere they went. Even the bands My Chemical Romance was touring with were quickly noticing the group's immense talent. Matt Skiba, the lead singer and guitarist of Alkaline Trio, a band from Chicago also performing on the tour, wandered out into the audience one night during one of My Chemical Romance's performances. "They were so good and sounded so great and the energy exchange with the crowd was something that I hadn't seen in a long time," he told *Alternative Press*.

A Chemical Romance Gone Sour

While the band was finding success with a mainstream audience, its members were facing increased difficulties. Gerard Way had a growing problem with alcohol and drugs, which only worsened while the band was on tour. He was drinking heavily and taking illegal drugs, all the while trying to hide his problems from his band members.

"Nobody in my band knew," he told *Alternative Press*. "I had a really good way of hiding stuff." What Gerard Way didn't know was that other band members had similar problems, including his brother, Mikey.

"I think I was accepting because I was equally as bad as he was at one point," Mikey Way told *Alternative Press*.

"Anytime you mix drinking with narcotics, something bad can happen," Iero added during the same interview. "And depression—mixing all three was really bad. Every time you do it, it changes your whole body chemistry. When we were touring, no one really thought about it, because we were all doing it together."

It was during this time that the band was scheduled to play in Japan, where they would have two of their biggest concerts ever. At the concert in Osaka, Gerard Way left the stage and got sick backstage. The mix of alcohol and drugs in his body was too much for him. Iero urged the band's manager, Brian Schechter, to get Way help.

Unhappy with how he was acting and the excessiveness surrounding him, Way made a decision. He got help, seeking the assistance of a therapist. He quit drinking, stopped taking drugs, and has been clean and sober since his return from Japan.

Marching to a Different Drummer

As Way and his bandmates focused on getting better, they faced another difficult decision. Unhappy with drummer Pelissier's performances, they were struggling to find a way to ask him to leave the band. But they all agreed it was time for a change.

"It was like the moment that you break up with someone you've been dating for three or four years that you used to love in the beginning of the relationship and things went sour, but for some reason you're still

After Matt Pelissier was asked to leave the band, My Chemical Romance invited Bob Bryar to become the band's newest drummer. Bryar was previously a sound mixer for the band the Used.

together," Iero told *Alternative Press*. Finally, Iero and Schechter went to Pelissier's home to break the news.

"People probably thought it was weird that we didn't make any kind of statement beforehand or really talk about what happened," Iero told *Alternative Press*. "It must have been weird for people to notice . . . one of the members who started the band and has been in the band for three years is now gone."

My Chemical Romance replaced Pelissier with Bob Bryar, the only band member who is not from New Jersey. A sound mixer for the Used, Bryar had been touring with the band. The drummer's personality and his performance skill meshed perfectly with My Chemical Romance, and he was hired after his first audition.

Three Cheers for Sweet Revenge had ended up exceeding everyone's expectations. The album sold in one week what *Bullets* had sold in almost two years, eventually going platinum and selling more than two million copies.

The band went on to have a great year in 2005, starting with headlining the Taste of Chaos Tour. They then served as the opening act for Green Day on the American Idiot Tour. (Green Day, a major American rock band that has sold more than

SECOND TIME AROUND

Three Cheers for Sweet Revenge is the band's second studio album. It was released in 2004 and was the band's first album with Reprise Records, a major record label. The album's songs include:

- "Helena"
- "To the End"
- "I'm Not Okay (I Promise)"
- "The Ghost of You"
- "The Jetset Life Is Gonna Kill You"
- "Interlude"

- "Thank You for the Venom"
- "Hang 'Em High"
- "It's Not a Fashion Statement, It's a Deathwish"
- "Cemetery Drive"
- "I Never Told You What I Do for a Living"

sixty million records worldwide, has been credited with reviving mainstream interest in punk rock.) During the summer, My Chemical Romance co-headlined the Warped Tour 2005 with Fall Out Boy and, later in the year, co-headlined and headlined their own tour.

Chapter Four

A Return to the Studio

After touring the country to promote *Three Cheers for Sweet Revenge*, My Chemical Romance returned to the studio to begin work on its next album. In the meantime, on March 21, 2006, the band released *Life on the Murder Scene*, a DVD/CD set featuring footage chronicling the band's history, the making of its videos, and a selection of the band's live performances. Though not compiled from new material, fans loved the new release.

The Black Parade

On April 10, 2006, My Chemical Romance—along with Rob Cavallo, a producer for many of Green Day's albums—returned to the studio to record *The Black Parade*. Released on October 23, 2006, in the United Kingdom and on October 24, 2006, in the

United States, the album was a departure for the band. It featured strings, horns, and a marching band. *Rolling Stone* gave the album four stars and called the work "a rabid, ingenious paraphrasing of echoes and kitsch from rock's golden age of bombast."

The single "Welcome to the Black Parade" reached number 1 on the UK Singles chart, giving the band its first number 1 song.

THIRD TIME'S THE CHARM

The Black Parade is My Chemical Romance's third studio album. The album was nominated for a Grammy Award for Best Boxed or Special Limited Edition Package. Some of the album's songs are:

- "The End."
- "This Is How I Disappear"
- "The Sharpest Lives"
- "Welcome to the Black Parade"
- "I Don't Love You"
- "House of Wolves"
- "Cancer"
- "Mama" (with Liza Minnelli)
- "Sleep"
- "Teenagers"
- "Disenchanted (Shut Up and Play)"
- "Famous Last Words"
- "Blood" (hidden track)
- "Heaven Help Us"
- "My Way Home Is Through You"

The album debuted at number 2 on the Billboard 200, with strong first-week sales of more than 381,000 units. The album was soon certified platinum, selling more than 1.1 million copies.

The Black Parade earned the band a number of awards as well. In *Rolling Stone*'s ranking of the top 50 best albums of 2006, *The Black Parade* ranked twentieth. The band won the award for Best International Band at the 2007 NME Awards, an annual music awards show founded by *NME (New Musical Express)* magazine. At the same show, Gerard Way won the Hero of the Year award.

Becoming "The Black Parade"

During the video shoot for the album's first singles, "Welcome to the Black Parade" and "Famous Last Words," both Gerard Way and Bob Bryar were injured. Way tore ligaments in his ankle, and Bryar sustained severe burns on the back of his legs, which required constant monitoring at a hospital. Because of the injuries, the band was forced to cancel a number of concerts, including an appearance at the Street Scene music festival in San Diego, California.

But by August 22, 2006, My Chemical Romance was back in action and ready to play a special show at the London Hammersmith Palais. The show sold out in fifteen minutes.

In 2006, My Chemical Romance performed at the Hammersmith Palais in London, England., a concert that sold out in just fifteen minutes. It was at this concert where the band unveiled its mysterious alter ego, "the Black Parade."

Many fans slept outside the venue the night before for tickets. However, when the show began, the band was nowhere in sight. Instead, twenty people dressed in black capes and with their faces obscured paraded around Hammersmith, followed by a large group of fans carrying signs that read "The Black Parade."

Shortly before My Chemical Romance was supposed to take the stage, it was announced that the band was unable to play. It would be replaced, according to the announcement, by a mysterious group called the Black Parade. Immediately, the crowd became hostile—until it became clear that the band was performing under a pseudonym, or another name. The band was taking the concept of its album seriously, performing in front of a backdrop of art displaying the words "The Black Parade." My Chemical Romance became the Black Parade, a theatrical version of themselves. They sported new, cropped haircuts and wore black band uniforms. Gerard Way had even dyed his black hair blond.

Touring the World

In support of its new album, the band embarked on the Black Parade World Tour during 2006 and 20007. The tour featured eighty performances worldwide, as well as several festivals and condensed shows. My Chemical Romance headlined the tour with a mix of both veteran and up-and-coming punk-rock bands opening the shows. For two months, the band toured the United States with Rise Against as its opening act. The band then flew overseas and took the Black Parade show to Europe. There, the band performed with Thursday and Funeral for a Friend. My Chemical Romance then returned to North America for more shows in the United States with Muse and the Bled.

BENEFIT PROJECTS

My Chemical Romance has been very involved in helping to raise money for a number of charities:

- KROQ's Almost Acoustic Christmas Concert, hosted by the Los Angeles–based radio station. The band performed at the all-day concert, which benefited Para Los Ninos, an organization that helps children living in poverty in the Los Angeles area.
- Concert for Tsunami Relief, hosted by K-Rock, a New York City radio station, and Music for Relief, a charity organization founded by the band Linkin Park. The band performed at the concert, which raised $75,000 for victims of the 2004 tsunami in Southeast Asia.
- Boarding for Breast Cancer, an organization that increases awareness of breast cancer. Gerard Way helped design a limited-edition blazer called "Prom Knight," the sales proceeds of which went to the cancer organization.
- Shirts for a Cure, which provides medicines and therapy to underprivileged women with breast cancer. Proceeds from a My Chemical Romance T-shirt were donated to the organization.

My Chemical Romance has donated shirt designs, like this one, to support Shirts for a Cure.

During the summer of 2007, My Chemical Romance took a break from the Black Parade Tour to join the band Linkin Park on the Projekt Revolution Tour. At this time, they announced that at the end of that tour they would be opening for Bon Jovi, an award-winning American rock band that has sold more than

The Black Parade performs at the House of Blues in Los Angeles, California. After this tour, the band landed a huge gig: it became the opening act for Bon Jovi, a mega-selling rock band that also happens to hail from New Jersey.

120 million albums worldwide since its start in 1983 and is also famously from New Jersey.

"I grew up as a Bon Jovi fan," Gerard Way told the *Maine Campus* magazine. "Whenever you're dealing with Bon Jovi or [Bruce] Springsteen, it's just a great honor and at that point, it doesn't really matter what genre you play. It really just kind of matters that you're all from New Jersey. It was just a huge honor to get asked to open for them, so we feel great about it."

When the summer ended, the band resumed the Black Parade Tour and played concerts in Mexico, Europe, and Australia.

Outside Pursuits

With mainstream success, four well-received albums, and a loyal legion of fans, the members of My Chemical Romance felt they could take a short break to pursue some outside projects following the Black Parade Tour. Gerard Way returned to his love of comic books and released *Umbrella Academy*, a six-issue comic book miniseries about the reunion of seven special children who were reared to save the world. He wrote the entire series, fulfilling a childhood dream of his.

The rest of the band took much-needed breaks as well. Mikey Way took some time off to get married; Iero returned home

Fans react during a My Chemical Romance concert at the DCU Center in Worcester, Massachusetts.

for some time with his family; and Bryar took a break to rest a wrist injury he'd suffered toward the end of the tour.

But with the band's stardom still on the rise, you can be sure that fans won't let My Chemical Romance take too much time off from recording and playing the music they love to hear.

Timeline

September 11, 2001 Gerard Way witnesses the terrorist attacks on New York City while working for the Cartoon Network. Way decides that day that he should pursue his dream to start a band.

July 23, 2002 My Chemical Romance's first album, *I Brought You My Bullets, You Brought Me Your Love*, is released.

March 21, 2006 A compilation album/DVD, *Life on the Murder Scene*, is released.

April 10, 2006 The band starts recording its third studio album, *The Black Parade*.

August 22, 2006 The band plays a special show at the 1,800-capacity London Hammersmith Palais in England and introduces the Black Parade, a theatrical version of itself.

September 2, 2006 My Chemical Romance posts "Welcome to the Black Parade" on its MySpace page, the first official release of the song to the public.

September 27, 2006 The "Welcome to the Black Parade" music video is released in the United States.

February 22, 2007 My Chemical Romance embarks on the Black Parade World Tour.

Discography

2002 *I Brought You My Bullets, You Brought Me Your Love*
(Eyeball Records)
2004 *Three Cheers for Sweet Revenge* (Reprise Records)
2006 *Life on the Murder Scene* (Reprise Records)
2006 *The Black Parade* (Reprise Records)

Glossary

Billboard 200 A list of the 200 best-selling albums in America.

Grammy Awards The Grammy Awards are the only peer-presented awards to honor artistic achievement, technical proficiency, and overall excellence in the recording industry. They are awarded by the Recording Academy.

heavy metal A genre of rock music that developed in the late 1960s and early 1970s. Its roots are in blues-rock and psychedelic rock. The bands that created heavy metal developed a thick, heavy, guitar-and-drums-centered sound, characterized by highly amplified distortion and fast guitar solos.

independent-label music Independent music, often called "indie," is a term used to describe genres, scenes, subcultures, styles, and other cultural attributes in music. It is characterized by its independence from major commercial record labels and its autonomous, do-it-yourself approach to recording and publishing.

internship A temporary position that emphasizes on-the-job training, rather than paid, full-time employment.

mainstream That which is ordinary or usual, with popular appeal to the masses.

NME Awards Founded by the music magazine *NME (New Musical Express)*, the NME Awards honor independent music. The first awards show was held in 1953, shortly after the founding of the magazine.

producer A music producer controls the recording sessions, coaches and guides the musicians, organizes and schedules production budgets and resources, and supervises the recording process.

pseudonym A fictitious name, also known as an alias.

For More Information

Canadian Academy of
    Recording Arts and Sciences
345 Adelaide Street West
2nd Floor
Toronto, ON M5V 1R5
Canada
Web site: http://www.
    carasonline.ca/index.php
The Canadian Academy of
    Recording Arts and Sciences
    is a not-for-profit organiza-
    tion whose main focus is
    the exploration and develop-
    ment of opportunities to
    promote and celebrate
    Canadian artists and music.

Rolling Stone
1290 Avenue of the Americas
New York, NY 10104-0298

(212) 484-1616
Web site: http://www.
    rollingstone.com
Rolling Stone is an American
    music magazine devoted to
    music, liberal politics, and
    popular culture. It is pub-
    lished every two weeks.

Web Sites

Due to the changing nature of
Internet links, Rosen Publishing
has developed an online list of
Web sites related to the subject
of this book. This site is
updated regularly. Please use
this link to access the list:

http://www.rosenlinks.com/
    cmtm/mycr

For Further Reading

Crimlis, Roger, and Alywyn W. Turner. *Cult Rock Posters: Ten Years of Classic Posters from the Punk, New Wave, and Glam Era*. New York, NY: Billboard Books, 2006.

Gale, Mona. *Inside Story of My Chemical Romance*. London, England: Omnibus Press, 2007.

Grossberger, Lewis. *Turn That Down! A Hysterical History of Rock, Roll, Pop, Soul, Punk, Funk, Rap, Grunge, Motown, Metal, Disco, Techno & Other Forms of Musical Aggression Over the Ages*. Cincinnati, OH: Emmis Books, 2005.

Haydn, Reinhardt. *My Chemical Romance: This Band Will Save Your Life*. Medford, NJ: Plexus Publishing, 2007.

Kauffman, Ronen. *New Brunswick, New Jersey, Goodbye: Bands, Dirty Basements, and the Search for Self*. Van Nuys, CA: Hopeless Records, 2007.

Robb, John. *Punk Rock: An Oral History*. London, England: Ebury, 2007.

Sinker, Daniel. *We Owe You Nothing: Punk Planet: The Collected Interviews*. New York, NY: Akashic Books, 2007.

Snowden, Don, and Gary Leonard. *Make the Music Go Bang! The Early L.A. Punk Scene*. New York, NY: St. Martin's Griffin, 1997.

Bibliography

Bruder, Jessica. "Loud New Jersey." NYTimes.com, December 18, 2005. Retrieved December 6, 2007 (http://www.nytimes.com/2005/12/18/nyregion/nyregionspecial2/18njCOVER.html).

Greenwald, Andy. "My Chemical Romance." Spin.com, May 31, 2005. Retrieved December 6, 2007 (http://www.spin.com/features/magazine/covers/2005/05/05312005_mcr).

MetalUnderground.com. "Interview with Gerard from My Chemical Romance." June 11, 2004. Retrieved December 1, 2007 (http://www.metalunderground.com/interviews/details.cfm?newsid = 8242).

Miller, Kirk. "My Chemical Romance: Album Review." *Rolling Stone*, July 8, 2004. Retrieved December 19, 2007 (http://www.rollingstone.com/artists/mychemicalromance/albums/album/6087106/review/6185205/three_cheers_for_sweet_revenge).

Rolling Stone. "Future of Music: Gerard Way." November 1, 2007. Retrieved December 17, 2007 (http://www.rollingstone.com/news/story/17168348/future_of_music_gerard_way).

Simon, Leslie. "Art Intimidates Life." *Alternative Press*, November 2004. Retrieved December 6, 2007 (http://www.theimmortalityproject.com/fansite/press/apnov04.html).

Index

About the Author

Laura La Bella is a writer with a diverse taste in music. Loving everything from jazz to hip-hop, from rap to country, she has been a longtime fan of the New Jersey music scene. She counts among her favorite musicians Bruce Springsteen and Bon Jovi. In fact, the first album she ever bought was Bon Jovi's *Slippery When Wet*. La Bella lives in Rochester, New York, with her husband, who is also an avid music lover.

Photo Credits

Cover, p. 1 Theo Wargo/WireImage; pp. 4–5 © Peter Kupfer/Action Press/Zuma Press; p. 9 © Aviv Small/Zuma Press; pp. 12, 26 Tim Mosenfelder/Getty Images; p. 13 Marcos Townsend/AFP/Getty Images; p. 14 Kevin Kane/WireImage; p. 18 Kevin Winter/Getty Images; p. 20 Lester Cohen/WireImage; p. 29 Chris McKay/WireImage; p. 35 Jo Hale/Getty Images; p. 37 http://merchnow.com/store/merchant.mv?Screen = CTGY&Store_Code = SFAC&Category_Code = MCR0; p. 38 Stephen Albanese/Michael Ochs Archives/Getty Images; p. 40 © AP Images.

Designer: Gene Mollica; **Editor:** Peter Herman; **Photo Researcher:** Cindy Reiman